BUYERS GUIDE FOR CRANES AND HOISTS

FIRST BOOK WRITTEN ON EOT CRANES IN INDIA

BUYERS GUIDE FOR CRANES AND HOISTS

FIRST BOOK WRITTEN ON EOT CRANES IN INDIA

Rohit Goel

Worldwide Published by

Pendown Press

PENDOWN PRESS LLP
An ISO 9001 & ISO 14001 Certified Co.
Regd. Office 3767A, Kanhaiya Nagar,
Tri Nagar, Delhi-110035
Ph.: 8180886000, 9650072927, 8595249536
E-mail: info@pendownpress.com
Branch Office 1A/2A, 20, Hari Sadan, Ansari Road,
Daryaganj, New Delhi-110002
Ph.: 011-45794768
Website: PendownPress.com

First Edition: 2023

ISBN: 978-93-5554-690-6

Layout and Cover Designed by Pendown Graphics Team
Printed and Bound in India by Thomson Press India Ltd.

Dedication

I dedicate this book to my father, Mr. Balraj Goel, for his immense vision, knowledge, dedication and contribution to society at large.

Starting from a small garage, he has built a successful manufacturing business that now has the capacity to design, manufacture and supply Huge Cranes of 200T and above also.

I would also like to dedicate this book to my trainers and gurus who have guided and supported me throughout my career, helping me grow and flourish.

Contents

Chapter 1

Introduction: To Material Handling Equipment

Chapter 2

Preparing The Requirement:

Understanding Needs & applications

Chapter 3

Preparing The Specification

Chapter 4

Buying Cranes: Major Input Parameters Required

Chapter 5

The 4 Step Framework:
Reduce the cost of your Buying Cranes

Why This Book?

In my journey I have seen many mistakes that buyers make, which ultimately leads to them wasting their money.

I have always contemplated how the financial burden and hardships of individuals purchasing cranes and hoists can be minimized.

To accomplish my mission of educating everyone and ensuring they are free from worries regarding material handling, I began conducting seminars on buying facts in 2018, and I am still continuing that effort. You can register for the upcoming seminar at.

https://www.revacranes.com/buyers-guide-workshop/.

However, I realized that my mission to educate 10 lakh people in the next 5 years cannot be solely achieved through seminars. As a result, I have made the decision to write this book.

This book is an extension of that commitment, focusing on the importance of educating users and ensuring that money is not wasted. It is purely written with the sole intention of mitigating these hardships.

About The Book

An EOT Crane or a Hoist is used in every kind of industry where there is a requirement of lifting and shifting material from one end of the shop to the other.

It could be a general fabrication workshop, a ship building workshop, or a nuclear power station for the maintenance of turbines or the handling of raw material in a small woodworking shop. It could also be a cleanroom application or a hazardous area where hazardous wastes are handled.

Every factory, industry or a plant requires an EOT Crane or a Hoist.

Being in the profession for the last 25 years, I have found that there are many misconceptions and myths surrounding the selection procedure and the applicability of cranes and hoists.

This book is written to guide buyers in selecting the correct crane or hoist for their material handling requirements, With the intentions of avoiding financial burdens and hardships.

I have tried to write the book in the most layman language so that it can be understood by a common man.

I recommend this book to be read by

- Design engineers who are working on projects to defining the requirements of crane or hoists.

- Civil engineers who are involved in designing buildings and layouts for plants or factories.

- Factory owners who are building new factories or expanding existing ones.

- Purchase managers and officers who are in process of negotiating and buying the cranes or hoists.

- Design engineers or other individuals who wish to learn about cranes and hoists.

- Maintenance personnel who have an interest in learning about the parts of cranes and hoists.

Rohit Goel (Accomplishments)

Rohit Goel is an expert in crane and hoist design and manufacturing, with a remarkable list of accomplishments, including:

Education:

- B.E. in Mechanical Engineering from Punjabi University
- M.Sc. in Mechatronics from Loughborough University, England
- Executive Education from ISB School of Business

Work History:

- Over 25 years dedicated to Reva Industries Limited, spanning roles in design, manufacturing, quality, PPC, marketing, sales, and systems development

Awards, Titles, and Designations:

- Director at Reva Industries
- Lean Manufacturing Practitioner - (Brand Ambassador by MSME ministry)
- Selected as a speaker in Zee TV's "Leader Speak" program.

Traits and Motives:

- An entrepreneur at heart, well-equipped to elevate businesses to new levels.

- Holds extensive experience as a crane designer and manufacturer, specializing in various crane and material handling equipments, and more, of varying sizes and capacities.

- Crafting tailor-made cranes for demanding applications like Nuclear Power, Hydro Power, and Hazardous Areas.

- Awarded the distinction of "Brand Ambassador" from the Ministry of Small and Medium Enterprises (MSME) for leading the Lean Manufacturing implementation in the manufacturing sector.

- Mission to cultivate "Highly Effective Teams" capable of delivering exceptional global client service.

- Aims to educate and share the common mistakes related to selecting, designing, and operating EOT cranes and hoists.

In essence, Rohit Goel's profound expertise in the crane industry uniquely positions him to provide comprehensive insights into Crane Designing and Operations.

Behind The Pen: Meet Rohit Goel

My grandfather, along with my father and uncle, started Reva back in 1963. Since my childhood, I had been hearing about cranes, the manufacturing process, advancements made, and the problems faced by customers. Cranes were discussed during breakfast and dinner, and I would often visit the factory, spending hours observing how the machines work.

I was very inquisitive and wanted to do something big, wanted to bring change in the industry and help whoever is associated with me.

In my teenage years, I developed an interest in Electronics and automation. I was amazed by how small IC chips could store vast amounts of data and, with the right logic, perform desired functions. I made many projects during my school time.

Computers were introduced in our school for the first time in 1988-89, which further developed my curiosity about how programming languages work based on logic principles. During that time, I learned several programming languages such as BASIC, C, FORTRAN and others.

For my undergraduate studies, I chose mechanical engineering to understand the basic concept of building machines and to explore my childhood passion for understanding how they operate.

For my post-graduation I chose Mechatronics. a field that combines mechanical and electronics. I wanted to pursue Robotics as it encompassed all my passions, utilizing my knowledge of mechanical engineering, electronics and programming.

During my MSc in England, I faced severe criticism from my German college mates. One day, our professor divided us into groups and announced that we would be engaging in practical programming of the PLC and constructing an AGV, with the best group being declared the winner. Unfortunately, I found myself in a group with the Germans. I spent the entire night reading about programming and was very excited to gain hands-on experience. But the Germans overpowered and criticised me on how an Indian can do such intellectual programming and made me sit at the side.

It was then I Pledged to myself that I had to bring India to the top. I had to ensure that the world saw Indians as authorities. I pledged to take my company, Reva, to such great heights that the world would witness how an Indian company could work wonders simply by prioritizing customer care. I pledged that anyone working or associated with me would be trained and educated, ensuring that they couldn't be fooled by anyone.

I joined the family business, Reva, and tried various ways to flourish and serve our clients and our team members. Through these efforts, my team and I were able to introduce advancements in cranes, which helps users as we work towards the "Fit and Forget" approach. We view Cranes as the roofs of a building, where any leakage in the roof or breakdown in a crane can result in significant productivity losses. I travelled extensively across the world, and visited major European and American crane companies, and incorporated the features and working methods into our cranes, all while maintaining competitive prices for the Indian market.

We at Reva take great pride in the fact that 78% of our turnover comes from repeat business. People often ask me why I don't invest in marketing advertisements to attract more business. My response is simple: I believe in working towards customer delight, ensuring that they do not face hardships, and that business will naturally follow when good work is done. I just want each crane we make to be better than the previous one. It should be more durable, productive and robust than the previous one. As a result, while conventional cranes often develop problems after 7-8 years of service, Reva cranes show signs of ageing after 15-20 years. This is our specialty and that is why whosoever takes cranes from us once prefers to come to us again. We even have cranes which have been working smoothly since 1987.

Recently, BHEL honoured our chairman, Balraj Goel, by inviting him to light the lamp and inaugurate their vendor meet, which itself is like a Lifetime Award for us.

My endeavour and mission are to ensure that no one faces any hardships when it comes to cranes. Your issues with material handling should not lead to mental harassment.

Acknowledgements

I would like to express my gratitude to the many people who have supported me throughout the creation of this book. I am thankful to those who provided support, engaged in discussions, read the book, offered comments, allowed me to quote their remarks, and assisted with editing, proofreading, and design.

Nobody has been more important to me in the pursuit of this project than the members of my family and my Reva Team. I would like to thank my parents, whose love and guidance have always supported me in whatever I pursue. They are my ultimate role models. I would also like to thank my teachers and colleagues who have been guiding me throughout.

Most importantly, I would like to express my heartfelt gratitude to my father, my mother, my loving and supportive wife, Anjali Goel, and my two wonderful children, Anshul and Sayesha, who constantly inspire me.

Last but not least, I humbly ask for forgiveness from all those who have been with me throughout the years and whose names I may have failed to mention.

Chapter 1

Introduction
To Material Handling Equipment

The equipment used for the movement of materials within short distances, as well as for storage and retrieval purposes, are collectively termed as material handling equipment.

This includes:

1. Conveyors and Chutes

2. Industrial trucks, forklifts, manual trolleys, AGVs/ mobile pick and carry cranes

3. **Over Head Cranes, Jib cranes, Goliath Cranes, Hoists**

4. Stacker Cranes

5. Tower Cranes, Articulating Cranes

6. Mobile Cranes (truck-mounted, rough terrain)

7. Fixed storage solutions such as platforms/pallets, storage bins/racks, etc.

8. Pallet load levellers, Turntables, Winches, Traversers, Lifting jacks, goods lifts, robot manipulators.

9. Custom-developed and other equipment which ease in movement, storage or lifting of the materials.

For the purpose of this book, we will focus on item 3, which includes Overhead Cranes, Jib Cranes, Goliath Cranes, Hoists.

Overhead Cranes/Jib Cranes/Goliath Cranes/Hoists

There are many types of overhead cranes and hoists commonly used inside or outside factories or sheds, with restricted travel or operational lengths. These cranes can be considered as fixed yet movable. This chapter describes the various types of overhead cranes, jib cranes, goliath cranes, and hoists, along with the relevant terminology.

What does EOT Crane stand for? Electric Overhead Travelling Crane.

What is the application of an EOT Crane/Hoist?

An EOT Crane/Hoist is a lifting device that is installed overhead, typically below the roof of a building and moving on rails. it is used to lift and transfer materials within a specified range or area in a workshop.

It is not a mobile crane, meaning it does not move on the floor.

It is used anywhere where the load to lift is more than around 50kg.

Cranes/Hoist are used in factories, workshops, plants, warehouses, sheds, godowns and ports.

How does a Crane or a Hoist work?

A Crane or a Hoist consists of various components, including a motor, brake, gearbox, drum, wire ropes, pulleys, hooks, structural elements and an electrical panel. It lifts the load using combination of a gearbox, motor, drum, sheaves and wire rope. And manouevers the load through a seperate set of motor, gearbox and wheels.

What are the different types of Cranes and Hoists?

- EOT Cranes
  - Double Girder EOT Crane {EOT stands for Electric Overhead Traverse}
  - Single Girder EOT Crane
  - Semi EOT Cranes -
    - Double Girder Semi EOT Cranes
    - Single Girder Semi EOT Cranes
- HOT Cranes
  - Hand Operated Double girder cranes
  - Hand Operated Single girder cranes
- Goliath Cranes
  - Double Girder Goliath Crane
  - Single Girder Goliath Crane
  - Semi Goliath Cranes

- Underhung Cranes
  - Double Girder
  - Single Girder
- Jib Cranes
  - Pillar mounted
  - Wall Mounted
  - Wall traversing
- Hoists
  - Electric Wire Rope Hoists (including Normal headroom hoist, Low headroom hoist, Bi-rail hoist, Fixed hoist)
  - Electric Chain Hoist
- Manual Hoist
  - Chain Pulley Block (CPB)

Double Girder EOT Crane

As the name suggests, these cranes feature double girders or double bridges, with a trolley or crab mounted on top. The trolley carries out the hoisting (up and down) and cross-travel motion.

The two bridges are attached to end carriages, which are equipped with sets of wheels.

A typical crane of this type includes:

- Hoisting motion (up and down motion) - (MH or AH)

- Cross travel motion (CT): allows movement across the span

- Long travel motion (LT): facilitates movement along the length of the bay

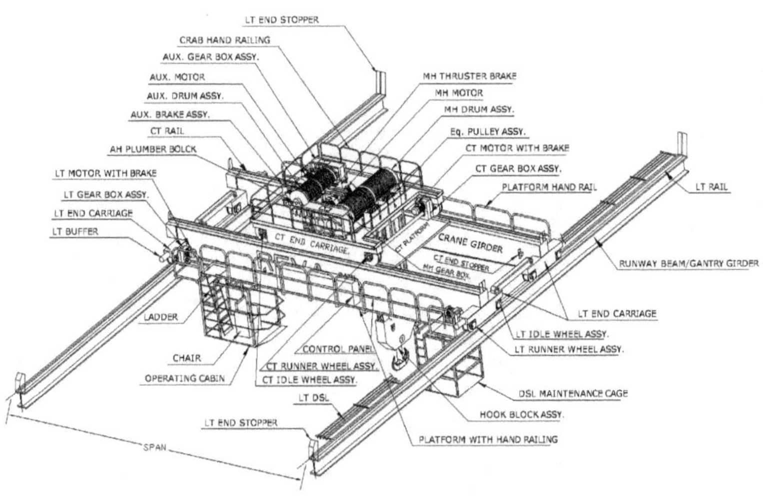

Double Girder EOT Crane

Single Girder EOT Crane

As the name suggests, these cranes consist of a single girder (bridge) with a hoist running under it. The bridge is mounted on an end carriage that carries wheels.

The wheels run on LT Rails, which are supported by gantry girders (runway beam).

The Runway beams, in turn, are supported on corbels attached to the pillars of the building.

Similar to the double girder crane, a single girder crane also includes all three motions: hoisting motion (up and down), cross-travel motion (across the span), and long travel motion (along the length).

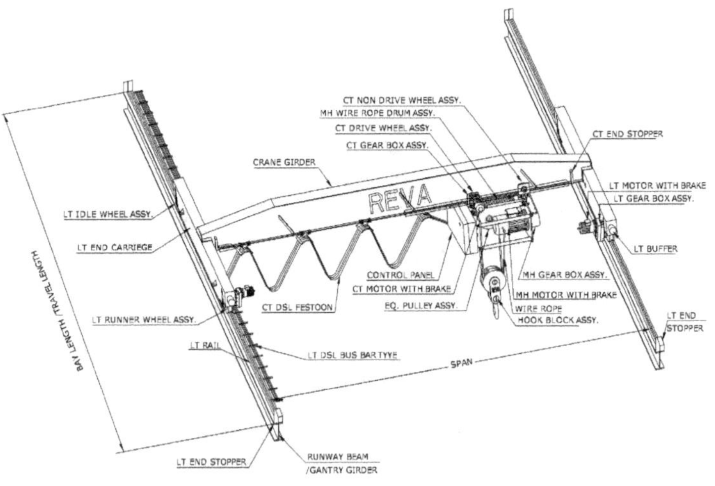

Single Girder EOT Crane

Underhung Crane

Underhung cranes are hanged on gantry girders, which are mounted inverted on trusses or beams.

They are typically designed for lighter weights and are specifically used for applications above a machine.

Underhung cranes can be configured as single girder or double girder, depending on the specific requirements.

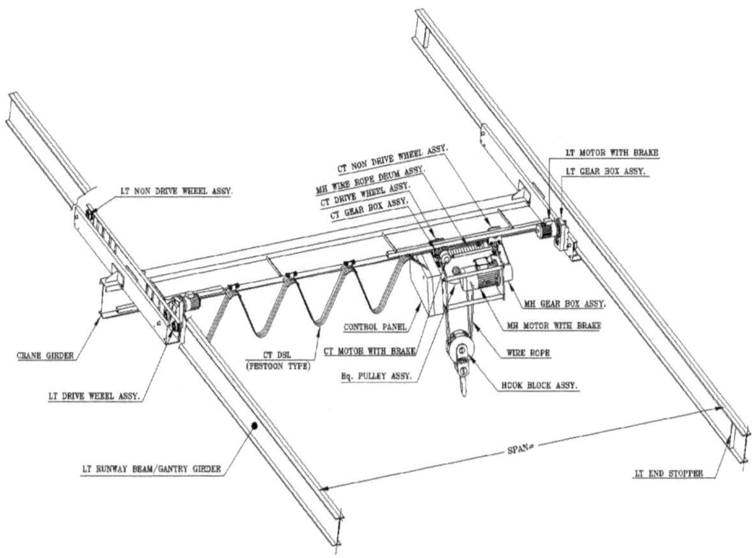

Underslung EOT Crane

Hoist

A Hoist is a machinery used for lifting materials using a hook, reeving wire rope/chain, and a drum/sprocket that is connected to a gearbox and motor.

By rotating the motor in one direction, the load is lifted, and rotating motor in the opposite direction lowers the load.

A hoist also features a traverse motion known as cross-travel motion, which enables the hoist to move along a fixed path (monorail), either with or without a load.

Therefore, a hoist typically consists of:

1. Hoisting motion - up and down

2. Cross-travel motion - movement along the monorail path.

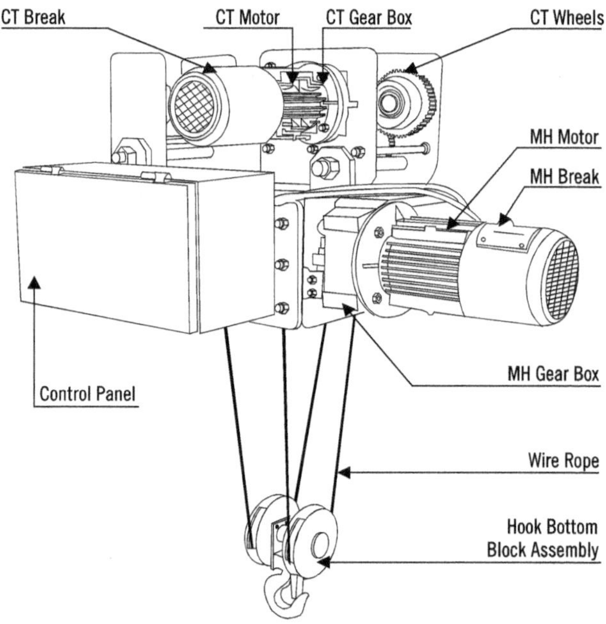

Electric Wire Rope Hoist

Goliath Crane

Gantry Cranes, commonly known as Goliath Cranes or Portal Cranes, are suitable for both indoor and outdoor use.

They are self-standing structures, (they are cranes with legs) and do not require support from walls or rigid columns of buildings.

They are majorly used in open warehouses or buildings where the column or structure may be weak. Or the usage is temporary.

Semi gantry cranes are particularly useful in situations where there is a building on one side only, and the other side is supported by gantry legs, providing additional advantages.

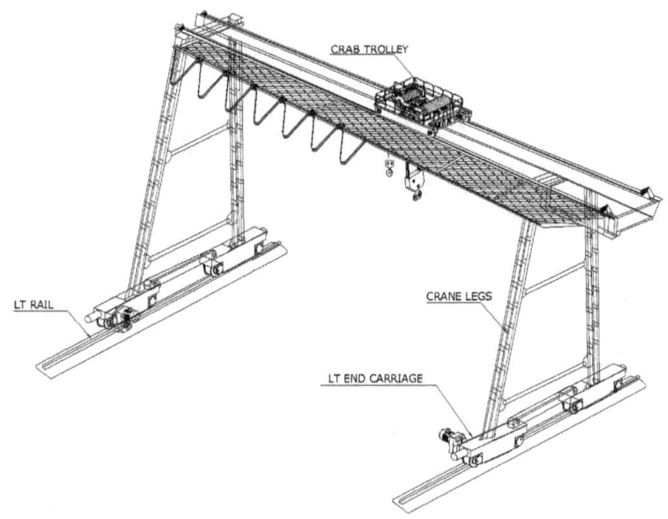

Double Girder Goliath Crane

JIB Cranes

JIB Cranes consists of a cantilever beam on which a hoist moves. There are different types of JIB Cranes, including self-standing, pillar-mounted, and wall-travelling configurations.

In the self-standing type, there is a pillar with a fixed foundation, either on the ground or on a machine. A cantilever beam is attached to the pillar using a set of bearings, allowing it to rotate about the pillar. The rotation could be 360, 270, 180 degrees, depending on the construction and requirements.

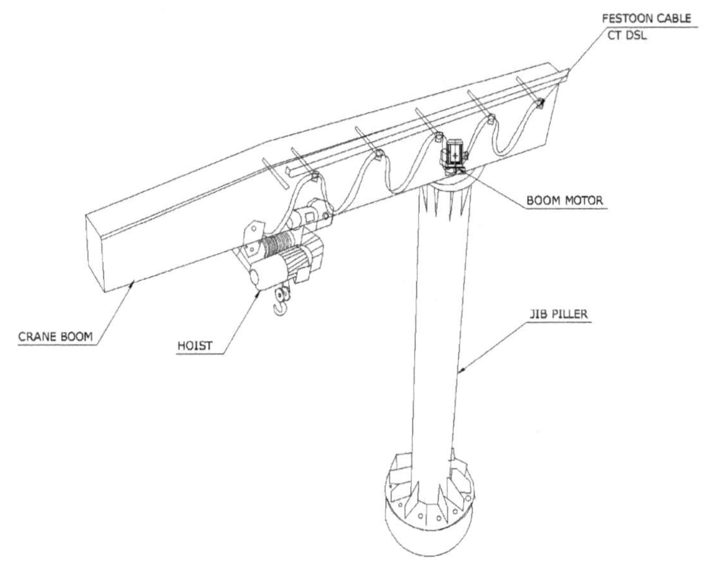

JIB Cranes

An electric chain hoist, or an electric wire rope hoist, or a manual hoist can be mounted on a jib crane.

Therefore, a jib crane typically offer the following motions:

1. Hoisting (up and down) motion

2. Cross travel along the cantilever beam

3. Rotation around the pillar

Chapter 2

Preparing The Requirement: Understanding Needs & applications

The better and closer you are to meeting your specific requirements, the more money and hardships you will save.

Following are the questions step by step:

1. Which kind of material handling suits my application?

2. Which overhead type to choose, wire rope hoist, chain hoist, double girder crane, single girder crane, goliath crane, or a jib crane? Should it be electric or manual?

3. What parameters to decide: capacity, span, lift, class of duty, indoor or outdoor usage, ambient temperature, operation speeds, motor type (squirrel cage or slip ring), VVVF drive requirements, micro-speed capabilities, and operation type (fixed pendant, independent movable pendant, radio remote, cabin operated - open/–closed)?

Which kind of material handling suits my application?

There are various options for material handling, as discussed in Chapter 1. Here are few sets of questions that can help you make a decision:

1. Should I choose a conveyor or an overhead crane?

Conveyor	Overhead
Pros	**Pros**
Ideal for bulk handling.	Ideal for handling one piece or a container.
Suitable for continuous process lines.	Suitable for lower frequency, irregular nature of handling.
Ideal where the material to be transferred is of fixed nature.	Ideal for flexibility in a defined area.
Ideal for small capacity but large volumes.	Ideal for a capacity range.
Ideal where material cannot be bundled in a bag or a container. Like flour can be conveyed from one end to another without putting and storing in a container, from one process to another.	Ideal where the material can be lifted with a sling or a attachment.
Ideal for in process, manufacturing process requirements.	Ideal for floor space saving, as it is installed overhead.
Ideal for automations.	Ideal for heavy loads.
Cons	**Cons**
Consume floor space	Cannot do Bulk hand handling.
Expensive	Is a comparatively slower process cycle.
Not suitable for heavy loads.	Not suited for automations.
Once fixed layout cannot be changed	Not suited for in process manufacturing process.
Capacity cannot be increased, once installed.	Require building to be designed for heavy loads.

2. Should I choose a forklift/industrial truck or an overhead crane?

Forklift/industrial trucks	Overhead
Can stack products up to the height of the mast.	EOT cranes allow greater hook height, enabling more efficient use of space for your business.
Forklift typically use gas motors or batteries, which have a shorter lifespan of around 5 to 10 years.	Use electric motors, which are more efficient and have a longer lifespan. Cranes can last over 30 years, saving your money in the long run.
In the case of a forklift, one operator is required for the forklift itself, and an additional person is needed to balance the load being lifted.	In case of EOT crane, one person can safely lift and transport larger loads.
Forklifts require regular maintenance and repair due to their tires, hydraulic systems, and batteries, which can result in added costs every few years.	In case of EOT cranes have electric motors and steel wheels that last for decades.
Forklifts take up valuable floor space and may not be practical when the production floor is already crowded with machines and items.	As EOT cranes are mounted overhead, they do not obstruct machinery or equipment on the floor. This allows for efficient movement of loads over the shortest distances, ensuring optimal utilization of floor space up to 100%.
Forklifts are typically used for lower capacities, mainly upto 5 tons.	EOT Cranes can be used from 0.1 ton to as high as 650 tons or even more.

Forklifts are flexible in terms of route, as they can be used to carry loads from one shop to another or anywhere within the worksite.	Overhead follow a fixed path of travel or operate within a specific area.
Useful for transferring loads between different locations.	Overhead cranes lack the ability to freely move to different loactions, requiring the use of transfer trolleys or traversers for such purposes.
Maintenance of forklifts is relatively easier since they are at floor level.	Maintenance of overhead cranes can present hazards, and troubleshooting can sometimes take hours. Additionally, the elevated mounting positions of overhead cranes can make maintenance work more challenging.
Forklifts are comparatively less expensive.	Overhead cranes require dedicated structures to support the cranes or hoists, which can increase the overall cost.
Forklifts are often readily available ex-stock, allowing for quick delivery and immediate use.	Manufacturing, installation, commissioning takes considerable time.

Once you have determined that overhead crane or hoist is required, you can proceed further with the selection and implementation process.

3. Which type of crane is suited for my application;

(a) Single girder or a double girder?

Single Girder EOT Crane	Double Girder EOT Crane
Single girders are comparatively more economical than double girders.	Double girder are expensive.
Both are equally rugged. Hence, it is a myth that single girder can used for light duty applications.	Double girder and single girder are equally rugged.
Maintenance hazards can be a challenge with single girders, as the hoist is hanging down from the girder and accessing it can be problematic. However, this can be countered with proper planning.	Double girder cranes offer maintenance ease as all components are typically mounted for easy access and maintenance. They also feature maintenance platforms for convenient movement during maintenance activities.
It consists of an Electric Hoist travelling on the lower flange of Main Girder, eliminating the need for rail for cross travels.	It consists of a crab mechanism traveling above both girders, running over cross travel rails, with a platform to maintain all parts of the crab.
Single girder cranes require more headroom than double girder cranes, which may result in increased building heights. However, by using a lower headroom hoist, this issue can be mitigated.	Contrary to common belief, double girder cranes occupy lesser headroom. By opting for a double girder crane, you can save on your building costs.
Single girder Cranes generally have no platform for maintenance, or limited to 2 small platforms for LT mechanism maintenance.	Double girder Cranes may have both sides platform across the main girders for maintenance purposes, including a platform for crab maintenance.

Single girder cranes do not consist of Under bridge lights.	Double girder cranes have underbridge light for illumination to work at night.
Single girder cranes can be operated using a pendant or radio remote, but they do not have provisions for an operator's cabin.	Double girder cranes can be operated by pendant, radio remote or operating Cabin or any combination of the above.
Single girder cranes typically have one brake per motion.	Mostly, double girder EOT cranes have EHT Brakes, and a combination of EHT and DC disc brakes is commonly used. This allows for the use of redundant brakes in hoisting motion.
Single girder EOT cranes are commonly used for spans up to 20 meters and capacities up to 25 tons in normal working conditions.	Double Girder EOT cranes can be used from 1 ton to more than 650 tons, depending on specific requirements.
Single girder cranes are primarily used in light applications for handling standard materials under standard working conditions.	Double girder EOT cranes used in all types of applications for handling material and even in very critical atmospheres like cement, steel and oil and gas.
Overall, single girder cranes have lesser weight compared to double girder cranes, resulting in lower wheel loads and the potential for smaller gantry girder sizes.	Double girder EOT cranes can be designed with an 8-wheel arrangement, which distributes the wheel load more evenly, resulting in a lighter gantry girder structure compared to single girder cranes.

Advantages of single girder cranes include:	Double girder cranes:
1) Lower cost 2) Lesser weight, resulting in lower building foundation requirements 3) Reduced freight costs 4) Easier installation process	1) Suitable for higher loads and spans. 2) Lower headroom compared to SG Cranes. 3) Easy Maintenance.

(b) Crane or a Hoist

Hoist	Crane
Hoist has primarily 2 directions of operations- 1) Hoisting - up & down 2) Cross travel - left and right	Cranes has primarily 3 directions of operations 1) Hoisting - up & down 2) Cross travel - left and right along the span 3) Long Travel - forward and reverse along the bay length
Because of the above, a hoist can cover only a predefined fixed path.	Crane can cover a complete area (such as a shed) as it offers 3 directional motion.
The hoist moves along the lower flange of a single monorail. No separate rail is required.	A crane requires gantry girders along with LT rails, which are installed on both sides of the building.
It is capable of manoeuvring on monorails with curved paths. Thereby, hoist can be used to cover the entire area in case it is predefined.	Gantry girders cannot be of curved path, although in certain cases they can be completely circular.
Hoist are compact and mostly standardised products.	Cranes are custom-made.
Hoist are more economical compared to cranes.	Cranes are more expensive.

(c) Chain hoist or an electric wire rope hoist

Chain Hoist	Electric Wire Rope Hoist
Chain hoist is compact in size.	EWRH Hoist is comparatively larger in size.
The chain hoist block remains the same regardless of the lifting height, requiring only the chain to be replaced when the lifting height needs to be increased.	The design of a hoist is dependent on the lifting height, meaning that a 12-meter 5-ton EWRH model could be different from a 16-meter 5-ton EWRH model.
They find their use in clean room applications or industries where avoiding contamination from oil, dust, etc., is critical, such as the food processing industry.	The electric Wire Rope hoists typically have oil-filled gearboxes, which can lead to contamination. Additionally, the wire rope used in EWRH hoists tends to attract dust and is difficult to clean.
Due to lower self-weight, chain hoists can be easily dismantled and installed at new location.	EWRH can be dismantled, however they are heavier than chain hoists.
Due to their compact size, they are suitable for areas with low head room available and where there are space constraints.	EWRH with low headroom options are available, but they cannot match the compactness of chain hoists.
Some chain hoists with single-phase motors are also available in the market at a much lower cost compared to electric wire rope hoists.	Single-phase equipment is not recommended as they lack built-in protections.
Chain hoists are useful for low-load applications below 3 tons, and with a lift height of up to 6 meters, where the frequency of operation is not high.	Hoist can easily handle loads up to 25 tons or more and lifting heights of 120 meters or above.

Ultimately, the cost of a chain hoist is much lower compared to an electric wire rope hoist due to its compact size and construction.	Cost of EWRH is higher but it is more reliable than a chain hoist.
Safety is an issue in chain hoists, as the chain can break in a moment, and can lead to serious accidents.	In the case of EWRH hoists, the wire rope strands break strand by strand, allowing for observation and replacement.
Frequent failures of the chain getting stuck in the sprocket have been observed, which can cause damage to the chain and lead to accidents.	EWRH is much safer in such situations.

(d) JIB Crane or an Overhead Crane

JIB Crane	Overhead Crane
They are generally installed in areas or on machines that require dedicated lifting such as machine, workstations or unloading bays.	Overhead cranes are typically used to cover the entire shed area.
JIB cranes are also utilized to maximize floor space in areas where overhead cranes cannot reach, such as the regions adjacent to the side walls of a shed.	Overhead cranes have side hook approaches, which means that the hook cannot reach the extreme ends of the shed.
JIB cranes generally have lower capacities With a maximum capacity of up to 10-tons and a boom length of 10 meters.	Overhead cranes are universal, ranging from 1 ton to 650 tons or even higher.
JIB cranes are typically more expensive compared to overhead cranes.	Overhead cranes are the most universal.

JIB cranes require strong foundations due to the significant overturning moments they generate. Let's say a 10-ton, 10-meter crane would create an overturning moment of 10x10 = 100TM, which is huge. As a result, the cost of foundations increases.	Overhead cranes are simply supported, meaning they do not develop overturning moments and only have direct axial loading.

JIB cranes are generally used in situations where overhead cranes are not feasible or where they are used in conjunction with overhead cranes to optimize the floor space.

Due to their restricted movements, JIB cranes are ideal for dedicated workstations, allowing users to perform tasks without relying on overhead cranes at all the times.

Additionally, JIB cranes are suitable for outdoor areas where overhead cranes may not be practical, such as loading and unloading from trucks that cannot enter the shed.

(e) Goliath Crane or an Overhead Crane

Goliath Crane	Overhead Crane
Goliath cranes are self-standing, overhead cranes with legs.	Overhead cranes require gantry girders, building pillars, and strong foundations to operate.
Majorly used in open areas.	Can only be used where building structure is present.
Can also be used where the existing building is not designed to support the loads required for overhead cranes.	Planning for overhead cranes involves designing the building, starting from the foundations, to accommodate the crane requirements.

Goliath cranes find applications where the load needs to be transferred from outside the span. The girders are extended beyond the rail span, allowing the crab/trolley to travel beyond the span and pick up the material.	Overhead cranes have limitations in terms of floor space utilization, as the hook approaches are limited to the area between the center of the rail and the maximum reach of the hook
These cranes are also used for temporary site works, where they can be installed and later uninstalled for shifting to other sites once work is completed.	Overhead cranes are typically planned for long-term usage within a particular shed.
The overall cost of the gantry crane system is lower compared to overhead cranes, as it eliminates the need for building pillars, building foundations, and gantry girders.	Compared to gantry cranes, overhead cranes require larger investments.

(f) Underhung or an Overhead Crane

Underhung/underslung crane	Overhead crane
Underhung Cranes are usually ceiling/roof mounted.	Overhead cranes run along the top of the column of the building.
Underhung cranes are hung on gantry girders which are mounted inversely on trusses or beams.	Overhead cranes are mounted on rails mounted on gantry girder which are positioned on top of the building columns.
These cranes are designed for lighter weights and are specifically used for applications above machinery.	Overhead cranes are designed for heavy-duty applications and can handle significant loads, with no weight limit..
Underslung cranes are often used in conjunction with overhead cranes to reduce the workload on the overhead cranes.	Overhead cranes are versatile and suitable for various applications.

The span of underslung cranes can be smaller than the width of the building, resulting in a lower cost.	Due to their mounting on columns of the building, the span of the crane is typically equal to the width of the building.
Underslung finds usage where the building width is high and only a small width requires a crane.	Overhead cranes can be expensive compared to other types of cranes.
Rails are not necessary for underslung cranes. Instead, inverted beams from the roof truss serve as the rail system.	Rails are required on top of the gantry girders.
Underslung cranes have a special application use for transferring loads from one bay to another.	The load transfer capability is limited to within the span of the crane.

Chapter 3

Preparing The Specification

Once it is decided which type of material handling equipment is suitable for my application, it is now time to decide the parameters based on the needs and requirements.

This chapter will help you understand the various parameters required.

How to select the capacity

The capacity of the crane is the maximum amount of load to be lifted throughout its lifetime.

Remember to include the weight of the slings or any lifting tackles below the hook.

There is a myth that cranes are designed for 125% of their capacity. However, this is not the case. The 125% figure is only for testing purposes.

Also, please note that there is no need to add or multiply any factors to the total load to be lifted. If your load requirement is 32-tons, Simply inform the crane manufacturer of the 32-ton load.

How to select the span of the crane

The span of the crane depends on the width of your building. Span is the center-to-center distance of crane runway rails, and it is not the building column center-to-center measurement.

If the width of the building has not yet been determined, it is generally recommended to keep the span of the crane within 30 meters. In my experience, when the span increases beyond 30 meters, the cost increases exponentially.

How to select the class of duty of the crane?

Class of duty selection is critical and is based on the average working per day of the crane and the total average life expectancy. The below table from IS:3177 helps in determining the class of duty.

The new classification of cranes   w coming into effect and the classification p esently in use can approximately be compared as follows:

Old Equivalent	New Classification	Average Working *Hours Per Day*	Average Total Life in *Working Hours, Min*
I	M1	0.5-4	400
	M2		800
	M3		1600
II	M4	4-6	3200
	M5		6300
III	M6	6-9	25000
IV	M7	6-9	35000
	M8	12	75000

Note: The unning time per day and total life relate to mechanism class only.

Please note that the above working hours of the crane are on full load, so in case the cranes are not subjected to full load always you may go for a step lower.

Further IS:3177:2020 annex B gives a detailed useful chart of application specific classes of duty to be used.

Further please do note that since now IS:4137 is superseded and merged in IS:3177:2020 it is important to understand and select the correct class of duty, as now the Hot metal handling cranes are M8 duty of IS:3177.

How does class of duty effect the prices? Are these important?

Yes, the class of duty is important in determining the lifespan and working hours of the crane. In standards, factors like duty factor and impact factor changes with an increase in the duty class. It is crucial to select the correct class, as choosing a lower class may result in the crane not functioning as desired. Conversely, selecting a higher class may lead to unnecessary additional expenses. For eg in the wire rope selection criteria for the value of Z_p is 4.5 compared to 9 for M8 classification, so there are huge differences and hence the difference in the cost also.

How to select the Speeds of the Crane

Crane speeds are an important parameter that depends on the application, performance requirements, as well as the cost of the product.

Speeds

- **Case 1**

  Normally, cranes are used for lifting and shifting loads. In this case, the load is only required to be lifted to a height sufficient for it to be clear of the ground, so that it can be manoeuvred.

  Or the actual lifting height is limited to 1-2 meters in normal working conditions.

  This means that the required lifting distance is very minimal, and hence, low lifting speeds should be sufficient.

  The traverse speeds, on the other hand, could be moderate in this case.

- **Case 2**

  For maintenance cranes or up to class 2 (M5 duty) cranes that are used for only 4-5 hours per day, where the crane's workload is not very heavy, low lifting speeds are suitable.

  Additionally, in this case, the traverse speeds can also be lower.

- **Case 3:** For production cranes where the application requires intense work and where low crane speeds can hamper the production, it is advisable to select moderate to high lifting and traverse speeds.

- **Case 4:** Application-specific cranes, Such as ladle cranes, liquid metal handling, 7-tank process, steel mill duty cranes, etc. require higher speeds.

So typically

Type of Cranes	Class of Duty	Lifting speed	Cross Travel Speed	Long Travel Speed
Erection/maintenance workshop cranes	Upto M5	3 mpm	15 mpm	20 mpm
Process/Production cranes	Upto M7	3-6 mpm	20 mpm	25-40 mpm
Application specific cranes	Upto M8	6-12 mpm	20-50 mpm	30-60 mpm

These are typical speeds based on experience and the user is free to choose any other speeds based on the past experience or application.

Should we opt for a micro speed?

Opting for a micro speed depends largely on applications. Below are some factors to consider when opting for a micro speed:

1. **Precise control:** some of the applications require precise movement of the crane, such as assembling parts or placing moulds etc.

2. **Delicate operations:** Handling fragile items, carrying liquid oils.

3. **Preventing swinging of the load:** High speeds during travel motions can cause the load to swing. To avoid this, micro speeds can be selected, and choosing a

VVVF drive is recommended for achieving micro speed control.

4. **Safe operations:** In case the bay is clumsy and full of material, it is safe to move the load at slower speeds.

5. **Cost:** Adding a micro speed will definitely add on the prices, so be careful while choosing the requirement.

How is micro speed achieved

Micro speed in a crane or hoist is primarily achieved through two methods:

1. **Additional gearbox and micro/creep/pony motor:** This mechanism involves adding an extra gearbox, motor and brake to the main gearbox. When the micro/ pony motor is activated, both the micro gearbox gear train and the main gearbox gear train run simultaneously, resulting in reduced speed.

2. **VVVF Drive:** If squirrel cage motors are used, a Variable Voltage Variable Frequency (VVVF) drive is employed to achieve slow, stepless speeds ranging from 10% to 100% of the main speed.

This has many advantages over the above mechanism. Please refer to this article for more details.

https://www.revacranes.com/ advantages-stepless-speed-control-using-vvvf-drives/

How to select the Lifting Height of the crane

The lifting height of the crane refers to the total hook travel in the vertical direction. Typically, it is measured as the vertical distance from the lowermost point where the hook needs to touch the ground to the uppermost position of the corbel where the crane will be installed.

People often make the error of forgetting to account for the height below the operating floor level. It is important to consider situations where the hook needs to travel below the operating floor level, such as in a pit or sump. Therefore, it is necessary to include the height below the operating floor level as an additional measurement, along with the height above the floor level, up to the corbel level or the rail line level. Taking this into account ensures an accurate determination of the required lifting height for the crane.

There could be different situations where you may find yourself unsure about the appropriate lifting height. If you encounter such situations, please do not hesitate to contact us or request a site visit.

Single or double hoist (auxiliary) configuration

The double hoist (auxiliary hoist) configuration is chosen when there is a need for tilting or a specific demand in the process that requires an additional hook.

Processes such as grab bucket applications and ladle handling do require an auxiliary hoist.

It is also considered when a user wants to lift or lower smaller loads at much higher speeds. This helps to reduce the burden on the main hook and enables faster handling of the materials.

However, the use of an auxiliary hoist should be approached judiciously as it can reduce the hook approaches and compromise the available floor space.

Should we opt for slip ring motors or squirrel cage motors

In the past, slip ring motors were preferred, especially for capacities higher than 10tons. This was because slip ring motors offer much higher starting torque, which is crucial for overhead cranes.

Additionally, slip ring motors provide speed control capabilities, allowing for the attainment of 4 to 6 different intermediate speeds through the use of resistances.

However, with the advent of VVVF drives, the combination of squirrel cage motors with VVVF drives is now preferred due to its simplicity and cost-effectiveness.

Squirrel cage motors have a simpler construction compared to slip ring motors. However, they had a disadvantage of lacking speed control capabilities, lower starting torque and high initial current.

These disadvantages are overcome by utilizing VVVF drives along with squirrel cage motors. The integration of VVVF drives allows for precise movements, and a stepless speed range of 10% to 100% of the designed speed can now be achieved.

Additionally, this combination is energy efficient. In slip ring motors, the energy is dissipated and burnt in resistances while using the slower speeds, whereas with the use of VVVF drives, the energy consumption is proportional to the speed and the loads being handled.

Should we opt for VVVF drives or direct online starting?

Using VVVF Drives is much more advantageous compared to direct online starting or using slip ring motors.

With direct online starting, the starting current can reach upto 600% of the normal current for a few microseconds. This produces a surge in the system, resulting in power factor loss and a temporary voltage drop. Such conditions are highly undesirable, especially when other machines are connected to the same power source.

Using VVVF drives have many advantages, which includes stepless speed control, the ability to avoid jerks and swings of the load, and reducing impact loads on the crane. VVVF drives also come with built-in motor protections like single phasing, phase sequence change, overcurrent, impact sensing, brake torque sensing, and more. For a comprehensive understanding of the advantages of using VVVF drives, please refer to the complete list of benefits.

https://www.revacranes.com/advantages-stepless-speed-control-using-vvvf-drives/

Which DSL type should be taken shrouded bus bar or angle iron type or festoon?

The DSL for the long travel motion have many options to choose from and user normally gets confused that which is the best and the right choice. The common choices are:

1. Bare Copper Wires

2. Angle Iron Type DSL

3. Festoon Arrangement

4. Energy chain

5. Cable Reeling Drum (spring type and motorized)

6. Shrouded Bus Bar

In earlier days, angle iron used to be the preferred choice. However, with the advent of shrouded bus bars, it has many advantages compared to any other type of DSL.

Shrouded bus bars are inverted U-shaped metal conductors in which current collectors slide and collect power. They offer several advantages, including:

1. Available in various current-carrying models: Shrouded bus bars are available in GI, Aluminium, Copper configurations, providing a wide range of combinations to suit different applications and current requirements.

2. The outer sleeve is made of PVC, reducing the risk of electrical shock or electrocution.

3. It is IP23 protected, ensuring finger safety.

4. It is inverted in profile, so the dust does not stick on the path of the current collectors.

5. Crane typically do not travel in a straight line, it shifts horizontally and moves in a zig zag manner. The current collectors are mounted on spring based pentograph and takes care of this horizontal movement of the crane. It saves disengagement of the current collectors from the bus bar and minimizing the risk of damage to the current collectors.

6. The same shrouded bus bar can accommodate the operation of two or more cranes simultaneously, allowing for efficient utilization of the infrastructure.

7. Shrouded bus bars offer ease of maintenance. In the event of bus bar damage, it can be replaced with a standard length of 4.5m, eliminating the need to replace the entire bus bar.

However, there are many applications where other type of DSL are preferred over shrouded bus bars. For example, in hazardous areas, festoon or energy chain systems are often used to avoid sparking risks. In Goliath Cranes, cable reeling drum is the preferred choice.

Should we opt for radio remote or not?

Radio remote controls offer numerous advantages, providing mobility and flexibility to the operator. It is important to note that, for safety the load should never be positioned directly above the operator. This is easily achieved using Radio Remote instead of a pendant. Radio remote finds usage in following applications:

- In places where the workshop or work area is highly congested, and it is not feasible for personnel to travel along with the pendant (attached to the crane), remote operation using radio controls becomes necessary.

- When the load to be handled is irregular.

- They are particularly useful when dealing with hazardous materials or hot metal handling, as they allow the operator to control the crane from a safer distance.

- Additionally, radio remote controls are advantageous when the load to be lifted is away from the operating area, such as a pit or a distant location.

- In a typical shop floor environment, a person can comfortably walk at a speed of around 50 meters per minute (mpm). However, due to obstacles and the need for increased attention in such environments, it is advisable to consider a radio remote control for crane operations if the long travel speed exceeds 30 mpm. This allows for better control and enhanced safety in navigating through the shop floor.

- It can be serves as a replacement to the cabin-controlled cranes.

- A single person can operate and hook the loads easily when radio remotes are used.

- Radio remote controls are extremely beneficial and cost-effective in situations where tandem motion is required, involving the simultaneous lifting and coordination of two cranes.

  The primary disadvantage of radio remote controls is the possibility of battery drainage.

Should we opt for cabin control or not?

Cabin control allows the operator to have a wide view of the entire shop and the load to be lifted. Usual cases where cabin is opted for are:

- The shop floor is highly congested, and there is no direct line of sight between the operator and the load.

- When handling heavy and bulky loads that require precise control and visibility, cabin control allows the operator to have a better perspective of the load and surrounding environment, ensuring safe and accurate lifting and transferring.

- In applications involving tasks such as hot metal handling or hazardous areas like waste management, cabin control provides a controlled and protected environment for the operator, ensuring their safety and minimizing the risk of accidents.

There are several disadvantages associated with Cabin-Controlled Cranes:

- A person has to climb up the crane and sit in the cabin for hours. This is a tedious task.

- Operating a crane requires the operator to have extensive experience and training, making it a challenging job.

- The operator must rely on hand signals and instructions from a person on the ground, which can sometimes lead to miscommunication or delays in crane movements.

- The operation of a cabin-controlled crane typically requires a minimum of two persons: one on the ground and one in the cabin.

- Crane operation becomes dependent on the crane operator, if the crane operator is on leave or unavailable, the crane remains unoperated.

- Cranes are subject to various impacts and vibrations, and these forces are transmitted to the operator sitting in the cabin, which can be physically demanding and uncomfortable.

Nowadays, cabin-controlled cranes are not commonly opted unless and until there is a specific application demand or requirement.

Which type of Brakes should be chosen?

Types of brakes and number of brakes are one of the important features to be considered for the safe operation of the crane.

Brakes can be classified based on three major parameters:

Categorisation 1	Shoe Brakes
	Disc Brakes
Categorisation 2	Electromagnetic Brakes - AC Operated
	Electromagnetic Brakes - DC Operated
	EHT Type - Electro Hydraulic Thrustor
Categorisation 3	Parking/storm Brakes

The Brakes used in crane/hoist applications are typically a combination of Category 1 and Category 2 brakes.

Therefore, the commonly used types of brakes for a crane/ hoist applications include:

Electro Hydraulic Thrustor (EHT) Type -	Shoe type	- Slow acting - High torque - Best suited for higher capacity cranes above 20 tons
Electro Hydraulic Thrustor (EHT) Type -	Disc Type (calliper)	- Very high torque. - Used on the output/drum side of the gearbox as emergency brake - Used in critical applications, like hot metal handling - Not commonly used
Electromagnetic Brakes - AC Operated	Shoe type	- High Torque - For high capacity - Not commonly preferred

Electromagnetic Brakes - AC Operated	Disc Type	- Medium to high torque - Suited for capacity below 20 ton or for CT and LT motion - Compact design - Economical
Electromagnetic Brakes - DC Operated	Shoe type	- High Torque - For high capacity - Commonly preferred in combination to EHT shoe
Electromagnetic Brakes - DC Operated	Disc Type	- Medium to high torque - Capacity below 20 ton or for CT and LT motion - Fast acting, when precise control is required, this is preferred - Compact design - Durable and long life

Preferred Brake types and numbers

Electro Hydraulic Thrustor (EHT) Type -	Shoe type	For capacity > 25 ton in hoisting motion. -2 nos
Electro Hydraulic Thrustor (EHT) Type - + Electromagnetic Brakes - DC Operated	Shoe type	Capacity > 50 ton in hoisting motion: EHT Shoe - 1 no + DC Shoe - 1 no
Electromagnetic Brakes - DC Operated	Disc Type	For capacity <= 25 ton - 1 no and in CT and LT motions - 1 no each motor

Underhung Lights are required or not?

Underhung lights are typically not required as the existing lighting arrangement in the shed/building is usually sufficient.

However, here are certain criteria and specific circumstances where underhung lights should be used.

Types of crane - in which underhung lights cannot be installed	- Underhung Cranes - Single Girder Cranes - JIB Cranes - Hoists
Type of crane - in which underhung lights are preferred	Goliath Cranes - as these cranes are normally used outdoors, there may be limited or no lighting around. Therefore, in such cases, underhung lights are required to ensure proper illumination for safe crane operations.
Type of crane – in which underhung lights are may be used	Double Girder Cranes - a) Check whether night working is required extensively. b) When the existing lighting arrangement is not sufficient. c) When there are chances of shadows on the load to be lifted due to the overhead shop lighting arrangements.

When to choose ramshorn hook?

Ramshorn	Heavy Duty: They typically used in applications that require a capacity of more than 40 tons.
	Load Distribution: Load distribution becomes a challenging task when dealing with uneven loads. However, with the presence of two branches in a ramshorn configuration, it is possible to adjust the slings to balance the load properly and expedite the process.
C-hooks	Versatile: Normally used for round/cylindrical or even objects.
	Ease: The shape of a C-hook is designed in such a way that load automatically balances itself, resulting in easier handling and reduced chances of slippage
	Size: C-hooks are smaller in size compared to ramshorn hooks, making them more suitable for use in smaller capacity applications..

Loadcell should be used or not?

Load cells are typically used to measure and monitor the load being lifted in real time.

In India, there is a saying that implies "a crane should be capable of lifting anything that comes beneath it". However, it is incorrect practice for an operator to determine the feasibility of lifting based solely on visual estimation of the load's volume. It is important to accurately measure the load being lifted using load cells, which provide precise weight information and ensure safe and efficient lifting operations.

Advantages of Load cells:

1. **Load monitoring:** Real-time monitoring of the load being lifted.

2. **Safe operation:** Load cells contribute to safe crane operation by providing warnings and tripping mechanisms if the load being lifted exceeds the crane's designed capacity (not allow to lift further). This helps prevent overloading and potential accidents, ensuring the safety of personnel and equipment.

3. **Eliminate use of weighbridge:** A separate weighing bridge is not required if load cells are used in the cranes.

4. **Data logging:** It can be used to store and record the data of load being lifted every time the crane is in operation. This feature allows for the collection of valuable data, which can be analyzed for various purposes such as performance evaluation, maintenance scheduling, and load trend analysis.

5. **Compliances:** It is good to have a load cell for the compliance and safety purposes.

Disadvantage/limitation of load cells:

1. It needs to be calibrated regularly, typically at least every 6 months.

2. If load cells are not properly calibrated or maintained, there is a risk of obtaining false readings.

Recommendation: All cranes with a capacity of above 40 tons must have load cells installed in them as a standard requirement. Additionally, load cells should be considered and installed based on specific application demands.

When should an Anti Collision device be opted for in a crane?

Anti-collision devices are typically non-contact (proximity) type limit switches operating on infrared rays. These anti collision devices senses any obstruction which is coming in the range and stops the motion.

In situations when two or more cranes operate within the same bay, it is essential to install anti-collision devices in both cranes, particularly for the long travel motion.

Normally, the LT limit switches in cranes are activated by limit switch strikers mounted at the end of the bay. However, these limit switches alone are not sufficient to prevent crane-to-crane collision within the same bay. To address this specific concern and avoid potential crane-to-crane collisions, anti-collision devices are used.

Limitations: The reflector needs proper cleaning.

Recommendation: It is strongly advised to have anti-collision installed when there are two or more cranes operating within the same bay, or if there are plans to add more cranes in the same bay in the future.

When should Encoders be used?

Encoders provide real-time feedback to the drives, conveying accurate information about the motor's rotational RPM and the precise position of the load being lifted (height of the load which is lifted).

Encoders are specifically used for the foll wing:

1. Precise control and positioning: Encoders are used in applications that require precise control and positioning, such as stackers and lifts. They enable the crane to stop at specific positions accurately, ensuring precise alignment and positioning of the load.

2. Tandem operation: Encoders are very useful in tandem motion, where multiple mechanisms need to be moved simultaneously at the same speed. By utilizing encoders, the load can be lifted and transferred without tilting or overloading one crane more than the others. This is done accurately by means of an encoder.

3. Anti-Sway features: Encoders along with VVVF drives, are used in applications that require anti-sway functionally.

4. Accurate speed: Encoders provide accurate speed measurement and feedback to the VVVF drive, which in turn can lower or increase the rotation speed of the motor accordingly. This ensures that the desired speed is maintained consistently throughout the operation.

5. Extended speed: Advancements in technology have made it possible to achieve speeds up to twice the designed speed during no-load conditions. This is achieved with use of special VVVF drives and encoders.

There are definite advantages to using the encoders; however, their usage should be assessed considering the associated cost. It is essential to evaluate the cost-to-benefit ratio before opting for this. While encoders provide valuable functionalities such as precise control, accurate positioning, and speed feedback, it is crucial to determine if the benefits outweigh the cost implications.

Should we opt for a platform or not?

Platform requirement: Platforms along the bridge girders are generally necessary for maintenance purposes. Due to the overhead position of the crane and limited or difficult access, maintenance personnel often encounter difficulties in maintaining the cranes.

As the designer of the building, it is important to ensure sufficient and easy access to the crane.

This includes providing a platform on the crane for maintenance purposes with ease.

However, it should be noted that platforms can only be installed on double girder cranes or on double girder goliath cranes.

Platforms cannot be provided on single girder cranes, underhung cranes or jib cranes for maintenance of the cranes.

When designing the shed, it is recommended to consider a fixed platform at the end of the shed. The platform should be positioned at a suitable level that allows the crane to be easily brought to that area for maintenance purposes. This ensures that the crane can be maintained effectively, enhancing its overall performance and lifespan.

Whether platforms should be provided on both the bridges or not.

In my opinion, having a platform on one side may be sufficient for maintenance and accessing crane parts. The crane vendor should ensure that the maintenance of all critical elements like CT DSL (Current Collector for Trolley DSL), can be easily maintained even if a platform is not provided on the non-driving side.

What is the normal time scale of execution of an EOT Crane?

One has to be careful about the timelines when ordering an EOT crane. The entire process, which includes understanding requirements, preparing specifications, getting quotations, finalizing and negotiating terms, drawing preparations, getting approvals for the drawings, manufacturing, inspection, painting, dispatch, transit, installation, and commissioning, requires time. It is crucial to consider these factors as they can impact your project deadlines.

A typical deadline for a 50-ton crane would be something as below:

Understanding requirements	:	30 days
Preparing specifications	:	30 days

Getting quotations and clarifications : 60 days

Finalising and negotiating : 30 days

Ordering : 10 days

Drawing preparations : 25 days

Drawings approvals : 90 days

Manufacturing of crane (min) : 120 days

Inspection : 15 days

Painting and dispatch : 15 days

Transit (depends on distance) : 20 days

Installation and commissioning : 45 days

Typically, a minimum of 490 days is required from understanding the requirements to the final execution and installation of a project. It's important to note that this timeline can vary significantly depending on the specific project requirements, complexity, and other factors.

Many projects experience delays and fail to be completed on time due to these lengthy timelines. Therefore, it is crucial to give due consideration to the time required for each stage of the project, from initial planning to final execution. Proper planning, efficient communication, and proactive management are essential to ensure that the project stays on track and meets the desired deadlines.

Chapter 4

Buying Cranes: Major Input Parameters Required

Crane Integral Parameters	Requirement
Class of Duty*: M1/M2/M3/M5/M7/M8:	
Capacity	
Capacity Main Hoist (MH) in T*:	
Capacity Aux Hoist (AH) in T:	
Lifting Height in M*:	
Span [centre to centre of the gantry rails] in M*:	
Type of Crane*: Single Girder/Double Girder/ Underhung Double Girder/Underhung Single Girder/Double Girder/Goliath Crane/Single Girder Goliath Crane [select one]	
Height of legs above operating floor level {applicable only in case of goliath cranes} mm:	
Speeds	
Lifting Speed MH in MPM: (Reva standard speed 3 mpm)	
Lifting Speed AH in MPM:	
Swivelling in MPM: (applicable for JIB Crane)	
Cross Travel Speed in MPM: (Reva standard speed 16mpm)	

Long Travel Speed in MPM: (Reva standard speed 20 mpm)	
Accessories Input/Parameters	
Brief details on the application of the crane	
Location: Indoor/Outdoor	
Area of usage: Normal/hot metal handling/ seismic zone/hazardous (atex)/high moisture/ high altitude/sub-zero temperature/high temperature above 50 degrees centigrade	
Gantry Rail Size in mm:	
Travel Length in M:	
Type of Motor in Hoisting/Cross Travel/Long Travel: Squirrel cage/Slip ring	
Main Hoisting	
Aux Hoisting	
Cross Travel	
Long Travel	
Creep Speed Requirement	
VVVF in MH: Yes/No | Pony motor required: Yes/No	
VVVF in AH: Yes/No | Pony motor required: Yes/No	
VVVF in CT: Yes/No | Pony motor required: Yes/No	
VVVF in LT: Yes/No | Pony motor required: Yes/No	
Type of operation*: Fixed pendant/ independent movable pendant/radio remote/ Cabin operated - open cabin/Cabin [select multiple or single]	
Type of Brakes required: Thrustor brake (EHT)/DC DISC/AC Disc/ACShoe/Parking Brake	

Type of CT DSL: Festooning System/Energy Chain/CRD	
Lights:	
Lights on the crane bridge drive side on platform: Yes/No	
Lights in the control panel: Yes/No	
Underhung lights: qty 0/2/4	
Type of Hook : C type / Ramshorn type:	
Anti Collision device: Yes/No	
Platform requirement: only drive side of the bridge/both sides of bridge/only small platforms on the drive side	
Load cells with load display: Yes/No	

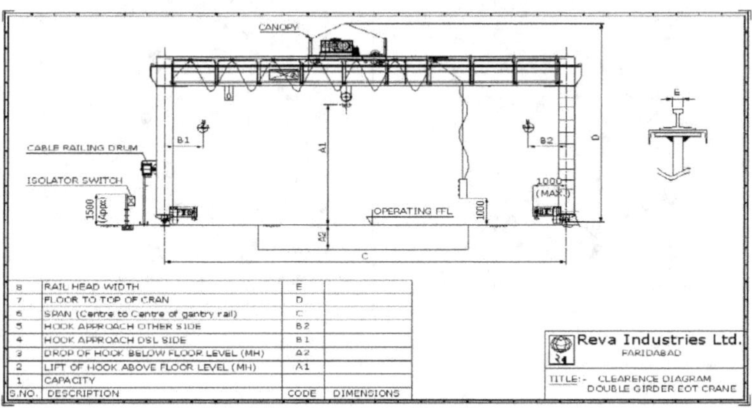

S.NO.	DESCRIPTION	CODE	DIMENSIONS
8	RAIL HEAD WIDTH	E	
7	FLOOR TO TOP OF CRAN	D	
6	SPAN (Centre to Centre of gantry rail)	C	
5	HOOK APPROACH OTHER SIDE	B2	
4	HOOK APPROACH DSL SIDE	B1	
3	DROP OF HOOK BELOW FLOOR LEVEL (MH)	A2	
2	LIFT OF HOOK ABOVE FLOOR LEVEL (MH)	A1	
1	CAPACITY		

You can visit our website at https://www.revacranes.com/ form/ to access the digital versions of these forms.

With our 60 years of experience, we have found that customers often get confused while filling these forms and the requirements. In case you feel stuck or need any help in filling in the inputs, do give us a call/WhatsApp us at +91 89298 96218, or you can mail us at mkt@revacranes.com. We are here to help and ensure that your requirements are accurately captured.

In addition to filling in the major parameters, it is necessary to prepare a specification document that clearly outlines the major specifications to be followed by the crane vendor.

To download the editable format of the specifications, click on the link below:

Electric hoist specification	EOT Crane Specification
https://bit.ly/Ehoistspecs	https://bit.ly/eotcranespecs

Chapter 5

The 4 Step Framework: Reduce the cost of your Buying Cranes

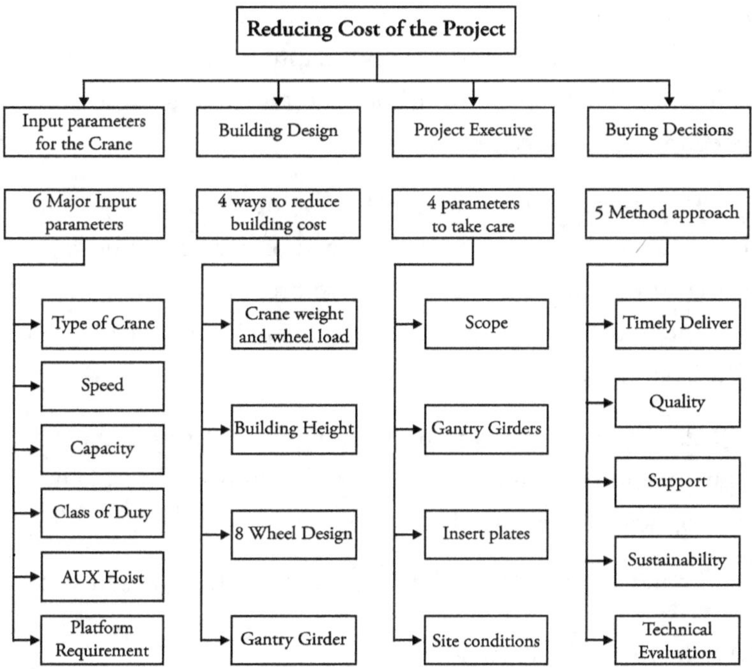

Step 1: Input Parameters

Input parameters play a vital role in determining the cost of a crane or hoist.

A) Speeds

The cost of a crane or hoist is directly influenced by its specifications, including the speed at which it operates. For example, a 5-ton hoist with a speed of 6 mpm speed may have the same price as a 10-ton hoist with a speed of 3 mpm speed. It is essential to exercise caution and be mindful of the speeds chosen particularly when it comes to hoisting speeds.

Please refer to Chapter 3 of our article, which provides detailed information on how to select the appropriate speeds for different applications. This chapter offers insights into various applications and outlines the corresponding preferred speeds for each specific scenario.

Also, please note that specifically for the hoisting motion the primary objective is to lift the load only to clear the ground so that it can be manoeuvred. Therefore, even if higher speeds are opted for the hoisting motion, it will not create much difference in productivity.

Also, it is important to note that lifting and traversing higher weights at high speeds are generally not advisable unless the application specifically requires it.

Therefore, it is crucial to choose the lifting speed wisely,

B) Selection of Capacity

It is important to avoid undue margins when selecting the capacity of the crane. Sometimes, designers tend to add undue margins to the lifting capacity for the purpose of safe handling. In certain cases, consultants may even ask for a 25% margin above the weight of the load to be lifted. However, it is absolutely not required and IS covers all the margins to be taken care while designing.

Yes, it is important to consider the weight of attachments like lifting beams or slings and include them in the total load to be lifted.

One should ask the correct weight from the manufacturer of the machine or the specific item to be lifted. Approximations can result in significant errors and compromise the safety and efficiency of the lifting operation.

C) Class of Duty

Class of Duty is an important parameter for reduction in the prices of the cranes/hoists. A lot has been talked about in chapter 3 on the class of duty also. The average working hours under full load has been mentioned for ease of determining the class of duty required.

D) Auxiliary Hoist

In most cases, an auxiliary hoist is not required and is often chosen based on the notion to avoid use of a heavier hook (MH) for handling smaller loads, or simply because the previous crane had an auxiliary hoist. However, it is important to carefully evaluate the necessity of an auxiliary hoist based on the specific application requirements.

Auxiliary hoists should only be chosen if there is a specific requirement for them.

In addition to the price increase, an auxiliary hoist also reduces the available floor space. And you are not able to utilise the floor space effectively.

Still, in case you feel that auxiliary hoist is a must, do contact us. There are many alternate ways of installing auxiliary hoists which will not be very costly and also will not occupy the floor space.

Also, with advancements in technology like the REVA CRANE BRAIN, it is possible to increase the speeds up to twice the designed speed. If you are interested in learning more about this feature, Please contact us.

E) Platforms

A short platform on one side is generally sufficient for maintenance purposes, particularly for cranes up to 30 tons of class 2 (M5) duty.

Apart from the price increase, the installation of platforms on cranes also increases their dead weight, which can lead to wasted energy during traverse operations.

Platform along the length of the crane should only be considered in cases where maintenance aspects are critical and pose significant challenges.

Step 2: Building Design

In addition to reducing crane costs, the overall project cost can be decreased by optimizing the building design.

I have observed in many places that while there is a tendency to negotiate and lower prices with the crane vendor, the building itself is often overdesigned.

In a few projects where we were involved from the initial stages, we were able to collaborate closely with the building design team and optimize the building cost to such an extent that the cost of the crane was completely free.

A) Crane Weight and Wheel loads

- Use accurate crane weights and wheel loads to design your building. It is observed that approximate wheel loads and crane weights are taken, which affects the building design. Ask the crane manufacturer for the correct weights.

  Please find attached Annexure 1, which includes a weight and height chart. Please note that these values may also change depending on many other factors, however, it provides a good approximation.

- Avoid taking multiplication factors. These are already accounted for in the standards. It is observed that the wheel loads are often multiplied to provide an additional safety margin.

  In the case of two cranes in the same bay, double the wheel loads are considered. However, it needs to be checked whether the two cranes will be loaded simultaneously on the same pillars or not.

- Opt for cranes with lower dead weights. In India, there is a tendency to buy cranes based on weight, which leads crane vendors to provide cranes with higher dead weights to satisfy customer demands. However, this results in higher wheel loads and increases the size of the building. Please try to reduce the weight of the cranes so that the building cost can be reduced. This can be achieved by requesting crane vendors to provide helical hardened gearboxes with gearpinions of low carbon alloy steel, hardened wheels, and the use of high-quality steel. These measures can effectively reduce the overall weight of the cranes.

B) Reduction in Building Heights

- The more the building height the higher the cost of the building as with the wind load and increase in height the cost increases exponentially.

- Opting for low head room design cranes and hoists is highly recommended. While this design is popular in Europe and other countries due to their concerns about building heights and the floor spaces, it is now available in India. By choosing low headroom cranes and hoists, significant savings can be achieved by reducing the building heights. In addition to the building height, the floor space is also very important. Opting for cranes with lower side clearances and lower hook approach designs is recommended. When selecting a crane vendor, it is important to prioritize maximizing floor space utilization. This leads to a higher return on investment (ROI) per square yard of the facility.

C) Opt for an 8-wheel design crane instead of a 4-wheel design crane.

The 8-wheel design distributes the loads more effectively, resulting in lower structural support requirements. This helps reduce both the cost and the dead weight of the gantry girders.

D) Gantry Girder

Gantry Girders should be within the scope of crane manufacturers only.

- The design will be optimised and suitable for the crane being supplied. Normally, if the gantry girder is supplied by a third party they tend to overdesign the gantry girder.

- There are possibilities of reducing the overall height of the building when both the gantry girder and cranes are within the scope of a single vendor.

- The straightness, levels, alignments, and joints of the gantry girder are crucial considerations for the performance of the EOT Crane. And, one must make the gantry girders and the long travel rails as part of the crane supply.

Also, it is not advisable to opt for gantry girders in a civil/concrete structure. There can be issues in alignments, and laying the rail becomes very difficult in such cases. Additionally, concrete gantry girders are much more costlier, difficult to install, and much heavier compared to steel gantry girders.

Step 3: Project Execution

A) Scope

- First and the foremost the scope clarity is crucial between the crane vendor and the client. Below is a table outlining all the probable items that are often overlooked:

Scope Matrix (Supplies & Logistics)			
Sr.	Description	Responsibility	
		Crane vendor	Buyer
1	Crane/s & allied items as per specs	yes	
2	Commissioning Spares (oil, rectifiers, pushbuttons) as may be required	yes	
3	Current Collectors		
4	LT DSL along with Power indication lamps at 2 ends		
5	Isolating switch (TPN) in each bay at operating floor level		
6	Cable (and cable tray) between isolating switch & DSL system		
7	Power termination up to ground station panel at supplier specified location/s in the Bay		yes
8	Long travel rail & rail clamps with needed fasteners		
9	Gantry girder (Steel/Concrete)		
10	Access ladder/staircase for Safe access to gantry girder from operating floor		
11	Gantry girder platforms & its' handrails		
12	Gantry end stoppers		

13	Loading of equipment on carriers at Supplier works		
14	Transportation of all the supply items to buyer's site		
15	Transit insurance during transportation of supply items from supplier to buyer's site		
16	Unloading of equipment from carriers at site		
17	Safe storage of equipment at site		
18	Any civil work		

Scope Matrix (Site Services: Erection & Commissioning)

Sr.	Description	Responsibility	
		Crane vendor	Buyer
1	Site related safety training and awareness during crane erection		yes
2	Work permit from competent authorities (If applicable in any state) for the workmen engaged at site		
3	WC policy/ESIC insurance as may be applicable for the workmen engaged at site		
4	PPE safety gears for workmen at site e.g. Lifelines, Belts, Helmets, Gloves, Shoes, etc.		
5	Clear floor space with adequate flooring free from scaffolding etc., for easy movement of vehicles carrying crane and parts		yes
6	Unloading of the crane parts from the carriers on shop floor before erection		
7	Civil modifications required, if any for installation		
8	Mobile crane, Hydra, Farana (F15) of suitable capacity — for erection of equipment		

9	Calibrated and tested equipment like chain pulley block, slings etc being used for installation		
10	Temporary power & power supply point in the bay for carrying out miscellaneous welding etc.		
11	Long travel gantry girder and rail installation		
12	Levelling and alignment checking of gantry girder		
13	Long travel rail installation		
14	Levelling and span measurement of the LT rails and gantry girder		
15	Main power cable termination at the isolator switch (operating level)		
16	Fixing of isolator switch, laying of cable and cable trays from isolator to DSL		
17	Providing earthing & earthing pit for bay		
18	Erection & commissioning of DSL system		
19	Erection & commissioning of crane		
20	Gantry end stoppers		
21	Power supply for testing of cranes (permanent power)		
22	Arrangement of test loads, slings & cradle for load testing at site below the crane hook		
23	Load test certification by Supplier, engineer and/or by competent engineer/local authorities		
24	Touch up painting of crane after erection if needed		
25	Touch up painting of gantry girders after installation of rails & DSL		
26	1 day Training to end-user's team members at the end of erection activities explaining crane, safe operation & Maintenance practices		

The editable version of the above scope matrix can be downloaded from the below links:

https://bit.ly/CraneScopeMatrix

Or scan this to download the crane scope matrix:

B) Gantry Girder

It is generally observed that the gantry girders are ignored during crane ordering, and the scope is not defined by anyone. In many projects, after the crane has reached site, it is found that the gantry girders were not ordered by anyone. This creates complete chaos. Preferably, keep the gantry girders supply within the scope of the crane manufacturer only.

C) Insert plates

In case the gantry girder is made of concrete, steel insert plates are required below the long travel rail, as well as for fixing the DSL. Do take care of these requirements.

Long Travel End Stoppers are also critical and are normally ignored, despite being small items. However, not installing End Stoppers poses a safety hazard.

D) Site conditions

Before the crane is reaching site the following should be taken care of, for faster execution

- **Site Route:**

  The site route should be surveyed and checked to determine if the crane can reach the site. If necessary, special transportation arrangements should be made or the crane vendor should be asked to split the crane girder or pack it in a way that meets the maximum dimensions.

- **Access to the building:**

  As a part of the site route survey only, it should be ensured that safe and clear access to the building is available.

- **Flooring:**

  The building flooring should be adequate and levelled to accommodate mobile cranes, trucks, etc., for easy entry into the building.

- **Roof open for installation of EOT:**

  The roof should be open at least at one end to facilitate the installation with mobile cranes. Discuss with the crane vendor if this is not feasible.

- **Levelling of Gantry Girders:**

  Levelling and alignment of the gantry girders are important for the performance of the crane. If the gantry girders are not properly levelled, the crane will skew, make screeching noise, and the long travel wheels will experience wear and tear.

- **Power supply available in the Shed:**

  Ensure the availability of temporary and permanent power supply in the shed. Install power cables up to the isolator switch.

- **Availability of Mobile cranes/Hydra at site/nearby.**

  It is important to ascertain the availability of mobile cranes/hydras near the site. Inform the crane vendor in case they are not available, so that timely actions can be taken.

- **Storage Space:**

  In case the installation site is not ready, ensure that there is a safe enclosed space for the crane to be stored, especially the electrical and the mechanical items (hoisting, CT and LT machineries).

Step 4: Buying Decision

There are more than 2000 crane manufacturers/fabricators in India, making the decision to buy the right crane is very difficult. There are vendors who are making cranes on road and there are European manufacturers also who have set up their base in India.

1. To make the decision-making process easier, we have identified a 5 Method approach to address this problem: Reputation & Experience

2. Technical Capability & Customisation

3. Product Quality & Infrastructure

4. After Sales Support

5. References

Chapter 7 provides detailed information on the same.

Chapter 6

Mistakes Commonly made while Buying Cranes

Top 3 things project personnel should note while ordering Cranes:

1. Ensure that the crane gantry girder and rails have been ordered.

2. Check if insert plates for mounting the gantry girders have been included in the civil design.

3. If the gantry girder is made of concrete, confirm whether insert plates for mounting the rail and DSL have been included in the civil design.

Others points to cross-check while ordering cranes:

1. Confirm that the EOT crane manufacturer is committing to the required time frame for delivering the crane to the site.

2. Ensure that the scope for load testing arrangements (load arrangement) has been defined in the contract.

3. Determine whose scope includes the arrangement of slings/cradles.

4. Verify that the scope for freight has been defined in the contract.

5. Confirm whether the site route has been checked and whether the crane as a single piece can be transported or not. If not, inform the crane vendor to make provisions for splitting the crane.

6. Ensure that the contract defines the unloading and storage area, as well as watch and ward responsibilities.

7. Verify if the transfer of the crane from the storage area to the installation place is defined in the contract.

8. Ensure that the scope of installation, commissioning, and handover has been finalized.

9. Determine whether the crane load test at the site requires the presence of a factory inspector. If yes, discuss whose scope it falls under.

Chapter 7

Selecting the Right Crane Supplier for Me?

Selecting the right crane vendor may be a difficult task. As the crane is a high-value equipment, and once installed it is expected to work for a minimum of 25 years. Therefore, it is crucial to select the right vendor for trouble-free operations.

Look for the following parameters in the crane vendor before ordering your cranes:

1. **Reputation & Experience:** Reputation and Experience are important factors to consider when selecting any vendor, especially when it comes to cranes, as they ensure availability of spares and after-sales service in the future. Look for a company that has been in existence for a long time and is expected to remain stable in the long run.

2. **Technical Capability & Customisation:** Cranes are all about customisation specifically according to your needs. Look for a company that has qualified and experienced design engineers. Check if the company offers software capabilities such as 2D and 3D

modelling, stress analysis software, gear design software, and crane design software..

3. **Infrastructure & Product Quality:** Infrastructure and machinery on which equipment is manufactured play an important role in ensuring product quality.

There is an old saying in Hindi

"जितना गुड़ डालोगे, उतना ही मीठा होगा"

Means the better the inputs (machinery and the infrastructure) the better will be the end results (products).

Imagine a part being machined on a machine worth 2 lakhs rupees and the same part being machined on a machine worth 20 lakhs rupees. Which one do you think would result in a better product?

So, before placing the order, visit the manufacturer and check their infrastructure, Verify the job work they are outsourcing and its source. Ensure the maintenance of quality standards, such as QMS, ISO and ZED certifications, within their system.

4. **After Sales Support:** After-sales support is required for any equipment, and it is especially crucial for electro-mechanical machinery due to the wear and tear that occurs. Check the after-sales service report and network of the company.

5. **References:** Lastly, the most important aspect is references. Talk to previous customers who have purchased cranes from the manufacturer and inquire about their capabilities as well as any shortcomings they may have encountered.

Above all, carefully compare the offers from different vendors, ensuring that all specification requirements are met. Compare the scope of work provided by each vendor and request the crane supplier to complete Chapter 5, Step 3, which details about the scope of supply, installation and commissioning.

Furthermore, compare the vendors based on the parameters listed in this comparison chart. If you need any assistance, please feel free to contact us at **mkt@revacranes.com**.

You can access the comparison chart at

https://bit.ly/CraneComparision

or Scan to download the crane comparison chart

Chapter 8

After Order placement

Your work does not stop after placing the order.

Typically, the following activities need to be completed after order placement.

1. Responsibility Matrix:

Ask the crane vendor for their responsibility matrix. Please share your responsibility matrix along with your email id and phone numbers.

The vendor responsibility matrix should include the following persons

Description	Responsible Person	Phone No	Email Id
Customer Relationship Mgr.			
Design Coordinator			
For Project Coordinator, Commercial and Despatch			
Manufacturing & Process Update			
Quality Assurance			
For Service & After Sales Support			

Similarly, you should provide your responsibility matrix, Including the details of the design person, quality person, execution/project persons, site person and post-execution finance person.

2. Execution schedule:

Request the L2 schedule for execution and manufacturing. If necessary, arrange a kick off meeting to confirm the timelines and discuss the responsibility matrix.

3. Drawing approvals:

This is one of the major tasks to be undertaken either by you or your assigned agency. It is crucial that the crane vendor incorporates all the specifications suggested in the form of drawings and submits them for approval, along with the necessary calculations to achieve the desired outcome. Please note that this is the stage where any discrepancies with the crane manufacturer can be identified.

Additionally, make sure to ask for the QAP to be followed during the manufacturing of the crane. A proper Quality Assurance plan is essential to ensure and maintain high quality standards.

If you need assistance, we can provide design calculations checking services of the vendor you have selected, free of cost. Please send the detailed drawings and calculations to **design@revacranes.com** and we will help you in ensuring that the crane is correctly designed and supplied.

In addition to design calculations, it is important to check the clearances to ensure they meet the site requirements. The span of the crane is a crucial dimension and should be measured at multiple points along the gantry rail to ensure the crane is manufactured accordingly.

4. Final Inspection:

Please make sure to visit the manufacturer's facility or assign a third party to conduct tests on the crane for overloading and loading, following the QAP and the guidelines described in IS: 3177. If travelling to the manufacturer is not feasible please ensure to conduct a remote video inspection. This step is important as each crane is customised and unique from the previous and should be tested.

5. Pre-installation site preparedness:

It has been observed that many times the site is not ready for the installation of the crane upon its arrival. Please refer to Chapter 5, Step 3, Part A, which provides details about the scope of supply, installation and commissioning to ensure proper site preparedness.

Also, please refer to Chapter 5, Step 3, Part D, which provides details about the site conditions that need to be checked before the crane is supplied.

Also, the following checklist is a must for timely execution

	Client Checklist Before Start of Erection & Commissioning of Eot Crane	
1	Levelling of Gantry Girder Has Been Done As Per Bs:466 - 1984 (Read This For Tolerance Chart https://bit.ly/CraneRailTolerances	Yes/No
2	Access To Crane Installation Site For Eot Crane And Mobile Crane	Yes/No
3	Flooring of Shed Complete For Shifting And Erection of Eot Crane	Yes/No
4	3 Phase + Earth 415V, 50 Hz Power Supply Available At Site For Erection And Load Testing of Crane.	Yes/No

The above checklist can be downloaded from https://bit.ly/CranePreInstallchecklist

6. Erection and Commissioning Procedure:

Proper installation and commissioning are necessary for the correct functioning of the crane and ensuring safety at the site during installation.

Every site is unique and requires a site-specific procedure for crane installation. This includes determining the necessary equipment for lifting the crane, identifying safety precautions etc.

Download this ebook guide for the general guidelines from https://bit.ly/CraneInstallGuide

7. Site Tests and Commissioning Report:

The EOT Crane should undergo testing without load, with load, and overload conditions. Also, the crane should be moved along its travel lengths to ensure proper functionality of the limit switches. All readings and observations should be carefully recorded in a comprehensive report.

Refer a standard format for the commissioning and handover report from

https://bit.ly/CraneSiteLoadTestReport

8. Operational Safety:

Cranes are machines, accidents involving which can be fatal to human life and cause damage to plant and machinery. The operation and use of a crane must be taken seriously and should only be performed by trained individuals.

The following are the points which should be taken care of as a minimum-

- Do not overload the Crane.

- If you are not sure of the weight to be lifted, please do not load it on intuition basis.

- Do not ride on or allow others to be transported by the crane.

- Do not play with the crane, always pick up load directly below the hook.

- Lift only a few inches above the ground initially, to check the functioning of the brakes.

- Stay clear while moving load, and do not allow any person to be under the load while lifted or under movement.

I humbly request that any new crane operator or rigger must receive training on operational safety before operating the crane. Therefore, please download the ebook and provide the necessary training to the operators.

https://bit.ly/operational-safety-cranes.

Or scan this and fill the details to download

9. **Daily Inspections:**

Daily inspections conducted by the crane operator are essential. The operator possesses a deep understanding of the crane and can detect changes in noises or any other signs of issues. Training the operators to perform daily inspection, at the beginning of each shift is highly recommended. You can download the daily inspection guidelines from the link below.

https://bit.ly/CraneDailyInspection.

10. **Periodic Inspections:** Performing periodic inspection, preventive maintenance, and upkeep of the crane is very important for the life of the crane and its performance.

Periodic inspection is not the primary focus of this book; However, I would like to empower you with the best information. As a gesture, I am offering a free e-book on periodic inspection of cranes.

https://bit.ly/CranesPeriodicInspection

Scan to download the e-book on periodic inspection of cranes and hoists.

Chapter 9

Technological Advancements

As technology continues to advance, there are also advancements in the field of overhead cranes.

Few Notable advancements are hereunder:

1. **Automation:** Automation has revolutionized various industries, including the field of cranes. Nowadays, there are cranes that are equipped to operate automatically, day and night, without the need for human intervention. These automated cranes are commonly used in hazardous areas or environments with high-speed and high-risk operations.

2. **PLC:** As a part of automation, the PLC can be programmed to operate cranes in Tandem. The PLC takes inputs from various sensors such as load cells, limit switches, and brake pad wear sensors, and others and instructs the driver to take appropriate actions or provide warnings. Furthermore, the crane's PLC can be integrated with the plant's PLC, allowing for information sharing and storage.

3. **Variable Frequency Drives:** Although they were introduced to India in the early 1990's, Variable Frequency Drives (VFDs) are now utilized in almost 80% of cranes. VFDs enable stepless speeds, motor protection, anti-sway capabilities, and more.

4. **Extended Speed Range:** This is a feature exclusive to VVVF Drives, Where the speed can be increased to twice the designed speed when the crane is operating without any load. It has been observed that cranes typically spend 80% of their operating time without any load. By doubling the speed during this 80% of the operation time, the plant's productivity can be increased by more than 2 times without any major investment.

5. **IOT:** The Internet of Things is now everywhere, and cranes are no exception. It is utilized for various purposes such as predictive maintenance, faults summary, overload and impact detection, greasing requirements, oil level monitoring, temperature rise sensing, and more. All this information is available on the cloud, allowing the personnel in the Crane Maintenance office to observe and monitor the crane.

6. **Energy Efficiency:** With the use of VVVF Drives, the Energy is consumed equivalent to the load and the speed at which it is being lifted. Also there are special VVVF drives through which every time the brakes are

applied to the crane, the power can be fed back to the grid, enhancing energy efficiency.

7. **Load monitoring:** Load cells are being used to monitor the load, providing real-time information and logging the weight being lifted.

8. **Remote Controls:** Despite being a technology over four decades old, radio remotes are now being used in almost 60% of the supplied cranes. Radio remotes serve as a superior alternative to cabin-controlled cranes.

9. **Optimised Crane Weights:** With advancements in Finite Element Method software and the availability of better alloy steel, cranes are becoming more optimised and rugged compared to before.

The ongoing advancements in automation, control systems, safety features, and material technology are driving innovation and continuously enhancing the capabilities of EOT cranes and We are delighted to be a part of this progress, observing and implementing these changes.

Chapter 10

Case Studies

Case Study 1

Regret the decision

Dinesh ji of HS Trading met me in 2016 and asked for a 35-ton EOT Crane for their new upcoming plant.

There were multiple series of discussions, meetings and site visits where we explored various ways to improve productivity and discussed the necessary features required to lift and transport the long plates cut from the decoiler.

However, Dinesh ji got a quotation from a local vendor and decided to proceed with them. After a year or so we crossed path at an industry conference, where he expressed his dissatisfaction with the crane and admitted that he had made a mistake by not choosing our services. He mentioned that despite the thorough explanation we provided about the design and machinery at Reva, he opted for the local vendor. He further shared that the crane was delivered significantly behind schedule and has not been performing as expected since its installation.

I told him not to worry and arranged a complimentary visit to audit and inspect the issues with the crane. During the audit, we discovered several areas where cost-cutting measures had been taken, such as using old gearboxes, smaller-sized hooks, motors of S1 duty instead of S4 duty, and poor-quality welding that appeared to be done by an unapproved welder. The evident lack of quality raised concerns, and it became apparent that 5 out of 10 machines produced by this vendor would likely encounter problems. In contrast, at Reva, we adhere to stringent quality standards. We manufacture our own gearboxes using low-carbon alloy steel, which are hardened to 55-60 HRC in our dedicated heat treatment plant. We implement 37 quality checks during the crane production process, and every crane undergoes physical testing at an overload capacity of 125%. Our designs are validated using world-renowned software, backed by our extensive experience working with over 9980 cranes till date.

Dinesh ji informed us that he intends to install another crane with the same capacity of 35 tons in the same bay. Surprisingly, within just 3 days, he placed an order for the new crane with us.

I feel disheartened that I couldn't convince Dinesh Ji earlier. It's not just about the money wasted; it's also about the time wasted and the hardships faced.

Case Study 2

Select the Right Crane Vendor

Nishant from GForg is a good friend of mine and has an export business with manufacturing operations based in Kolkata.

In 2019, Nishant needed to purchase a double girder crane with a 6-ton capacity and a 17-meter span. We discussed the requirements and all the technical parameters, including the need for VVVF drives, the type of gearboxes, wheel sizes, platforms, motor KW, and detailed specifications. Nishant got quotes from various parties, including local suppliers from Howrah.

Nishant decided to proceed with the local parties as their cost were lower, and he also considered the additional freight expenses from our end. I assured Nishant that it was not an issue and provided him with further tips to ensure smooth execution of the project.

A few months later, Nishant called me in distress, explaining that his crane was experiencing breakdowns every two days. I was genuinely surprised as a new crane should not be performing in such a manner. I assured him that we would send our technicians to assess the situation and try to resolve the problem. Our technicians visited the site, to our surprise, we found substandard parts were being used. For instance, the hoisting motion was achieved using a hoist instead of an industrial trolley. The hoist was made as per is: 3938 and was not suitable for is; 3177. Also, the hoist had a ¼ fall configuration and the load was n ot equally distributed on both girders. Furthermore, the limit switches were of the micro switch type instead of industrial-grade switches.

With our interventions and a few changes to the parts, we were able to make the crane operational and resolve their immediate issues. However, there were still numerous substandard items that could not be replaced.

After that, Nishant frequently called to express his dissatisfaction with the crane's performance and the lack of support from the other party. I feel stressed and demoralized that my mission of India being at the forefront globally is being hindered by significant production losses in terms of time and money caused by malfunctioning overhead cranes.

Case Study 3

Save Money

Gupta ji of Mongers Pvt Ltd. approached us with a requirement for three cranes for their new plant.

Specifically, they needed a 25/5-ton crane with an 18.5-meter span. During our discussions, we questioned the need for an auxiliary hoist. The usual response was that the 5-ton auxiliary hoist was necessary for lifting lighter loads at higher speeds, without having to engage the larger 25-ton motors. Additionally, Gupta Ji emphasized the importance of space utilization in their shed and sought an economical and practical solution.

During our discussions, we suggested to Gupta Ji that they remove the auxiliary hoist and opt for Reva Crane Brain, which would allow them to double the speed of the main hoist motor when operating with no load. We also explained that with the VVVF Drive, the current consumed is equivalent to the load being handled. Therefore, if they are lifting only a 5 ton load with a 25-ton motor, the corresponding current will only be consumed for that load.

We further clarified that removing the auxiliary hoist would not only save them approximately Rs 5 lakhs in cost but also increase the space utilisation of their shed. Gupta Ji readily accepted this suggestion.

Gupta ji was happy with the decisions and thanked me for the advice and saving money for them.

Annexure 1

Chart of the Dimensions of a Double Girder EOT Crane

SWL (T)	Span (M)	LT Wheel Base (MM)	Top of Crane from Runway Rail (MM)	Crane Weight (T)	LT Wheel Load for 8 Wheel (T)
15	5	2900	1600	6.74	3.58
15	7.5	2900	1700	8.72	4.15
15	10	3050	1800	10.69	4.57
15	12.5	3050	2000	12.12	4.92
15	15	3100	2100	13.14	5.24
15	20	3350	2400	18.26	5.83
15	25	3600	2600	22.96	4.4
20	65	2850	1700	7.8	4.55
20	7.5	2900	1900	8.69	5.29
20	10	2950	2050	11.06	5.79
20	12.5	3000	2100	13.1	6.23
20	15	3000	2400	15.2	6.55
20	20	3350	2500	20.3	7.35
20	25	3600	2700	25.99	7.97
25	5	2950	1800	8.78	5.55
25	7.5	3200	1900	10.04	6.46
25	10	3050	2100	14.02	7.03
25	12.5	3350	2200	15.36	7.53
25	15	3150	2400	16.28	7.88

25	20	3450	2450	21.09	8.75
25	25	3650	2700	26.96	9.61
30	5	2800	1800	10.81	6.66
30	7.5	2850	1900	12.76	7.78
30	10	2900	2100	15.04	8.49
30	12.5	2950	2200	17.31	9.07
30	15	2900	2500	19.82	9.56
30	20	3350	2550	25.69	10.57
30	25	3600	2750	37.62	24.03
50	10	3550	2200	18.27	13.33
50	15	3600	2500	24.7	14.9
50	20	3700	2600	32.1	16.23
50	25	3900	2800	43.46	17.8
75	15	4500	3000	31.65	21.1
75	20	4650	3200	40.05	23.8
75	25	4850	3250	51.88	24.74

For full chart of Wheel Loads and Crane Weights:

https://bit.ly/CraneWheelLoadWeight

This is Approx data considered on ideal conditions. It may change during final engineering.

Conclusion

The process of Crane Buying and Execution involves the following steps:

1. Understand which type of Crane/Hoist is best suited for my application.

2. Prepare the specifications and the parameters - involve us at this stage.

3. Each parameter has a cost linked to it.

4. Building costs can be reduced with correct crane heights, weights and wheel loads.

5. Ensure that the Scope is clearly defined and accepted.

6. Select the Right Crane Supplier.

7. Ensure site conditions and readiness.

8. Maintain the Crane.

So, What's Next

I understand the challenges people face when ordering cranes and hoists, and I am determined to address their concerns.

Although, I usually have limited availability, I appreciate your willingness to learn more by reading this book. I am committed to being available for your queries and discussing ways we can collectively reduce the project's cost. Do write to me at **rohit@revacranes.com,** and our team will arrange a Zoom meeting for you to connect with me.

www.ingramcontent.com/pod-product-compliance
Lightning Source LLC
LaVergne TN
LVHW010649200726
843507LV00011B/1790